BERTOLT BRECHT
LOVE POEMS

BERTOLT BRECHT
LOVE
POEMS

Translated by
David Constantine and Tom Kuhn

Foreword by Barbara Brecht-Schall

LIVERIGHT PUBLISHING CORPORATION
A Division of
W. W. NORTON & COMPANY
NEW YORK | LONDON

Portrait of Bertolt Brecht (1931) by Paul Hamann, © *Chris Drinkwater 2014.*

Acknowledgments are due to the editors of the following publications,
in which some of these poems first appeared: *Modern Poetry
in Translation, The New Yorker.*

For information about permission to reproduce selections from this book,
write to Permissions, Liveright Publishing Corporation, a division of
W. W. Norton & Company, Inc., 500 Fifth Avenue, New York, NY 10110

For information about special discounts for bulk purchases, please contact
W. W. Norton Special Sales at specialsales@wwnorton.com or 800-233-4830

Manufacturing by Courier Westford
Book design by Brook Koven
Production managers: Devon Zahn and Ruth Toda

Library of Congress Cataloging-in-Publication Data

Brecht, Bertolt, 1898–1956.
[Poems. Selections English]
Love Poems / Bertolt Brecht ; translated by David Constantine
and Tom Kuhn ; foreword by Barbara Brecht-Schall. — First edition.
pages cm
Includes bibliographical references.
ISBN 978-0-87140-856-3 (hardcover)
I. Constantine, David, 1944– translator.
II. Kuhn, Tom, translator. III. Title.
PT2603.R397A2 2015
831'.912—dc23

2014026214

Liveright Publishing Corporation
500 Fifth Avenue, New York, N.Y. 10110
www.wwnorton.com

W. W. Norton & Company Ltd.
Castle House, 75/76 Wells Street, London W1T 3QT

1 2 3 4 5 6 7 8 9 0

CONTENTS

Contents

A PERSONAL FOREWORD

P apa loved women, many women. Anyone who knew him would not dispute this fact, and he was faithful to each of them. I still do not understand the attraction that they felt for him. To be completely honest, Bidi—the nickname that I used for him, a name he had acquired as a little boy in Augsburg— did not wash enough and wore long underwear, well after it was fashionable. But even as a young girl, I remember that women, like flies to honey, would always find him witty and charming. His passion, whether expressed to women, to his art, or to his children, seemed all-encompassing.

In now reflecting on my father, who died when I was twenty-six, this love, which formed so mammoth a part of his being, was most keenly expressed, I believe, in his poems. Yet my father, who as Hannah Arendt once wrote "staked his life and his art as few poets have ever done," curiously remains far better known for his plays than for his poetry, especially in English-speaking countries. At the time of his death in 1956, no one, including my mother, Helene Weigel (she would call him "Brecht," never "Bidi"), had any idea just how many poems he had written, but today we know that he composed over two thousand that encompass the totality of human existence— from nature to politics, including, quite prominently, love and sex. These poems, when they eventually appeared in

Germany, became an enormous success, but initially it was not easy to get the love poems published, especially those whose explicitness created some hesitation at the time.

Even as a young girl, I always loved the poems. I remember him writing in the morning on several desks, since he had so many other things simultaneously going on. He was not, you might say, the type to take a shower before breakfast, but would simply put his trousers over his nightshirt and appear in our kitchen, then in Santa Monica, where we lived in the later years of the war, in a white clapboard house at 1063 Twenty-sixth Street. I would get him a cup of coffee or tea, but then he would start working immediately, whether at poetry or plays. I've been asked if he read his poems out loud to the family, which he would do only occasionally, very occasionally, only when he'd need a rhyme and would ask me for one, or if we happened to have guests.

From the time I was little, I felt immensely spoiled by my parents, who went to great lengths to make sure that I felt special. Nothing demonstrates this more than the story of our family's escape from Germany in February of 1933. Just as the Reichstag burned down, Papa lay in the hospital in Berlin, recovering from appendicitis. My mother went to his room and asked what they should do, and he told her they must leave immediately. Perhaps just as serious as his condition was the fact that I was not in Berlin, but with my grandfather in Augsburg. The situation appeared so dire that they could not even wait for me. Even though he was hardly recovered, they left the hospital and took the next train to Vienna, still five years away from the *Anschluss*. The problem remained how to squire me, a little girl, out of a country whose borders were now patrolled and sealed. Arriving in the Austrian capital, they met up with Irene Grant, an English woman and a Quaker, who had a passport not only for herself but for her young son. It could not have been more perfect. She agreed to help, so I, a three-year-old girl, left Germany as a four-year-old boy, and was reunited immediately with my hugely relieved parents, who then promptly left Austria. We did not go far though, settling in Copenhagen, because my father wanted to remain geographically close to Germany, believing that the German people would come to their senses and soon toss the Nazis out of power.

In 1940, seven agonizing years later, we had, it seemed, become a family of permanent exile. Rather than having returned proudly to a restored democratic country, we continued to languish in Denmark, the situation far worse than anyone had imagined. Germany had already invaded Poland, England and France had declared war on the Nazis, and by this time the Danish-German border was anything but secure. You'd think that given the gravity of the political situation as well as the parade of refugee artists and visitors who needed to see Papa, he would have known little about my inner life, but an essay, which he simply called "Barbara," written some time while in Denmark in 1940, suggests just the opposite. "Barbara—ten years old—is as thin as a sparrow in March," he writes of this bookworm of a daughter, who even then found chocolate wonderful. "She has a tiny face with vibrant blue eyes," he observes. "She is a strange creation, wild as a small hurricane, tender as Belgian lace. She can almost draw blood with her questions and is particularly generous in voicing her opinions." Even though I've always thought that I take far more after my mother, I have to admit that the occasionally irascible, sensitive free spirit whom he describes as his daughter may take far more after him than I might care to admit.

Our lives as exiles continued to pose challenges, long after our move to the States and even after the end of the war, but Papa always went back to his poetry, which clearly must have been very important to him, since it took up so much of his time. My mother, Helene Weigel Brecht, who after our return to Berlin was one of the great actresses in the world and was known to everyone as Heli, recognized the value of his poetic work. In addition to looking after Papa's Berliner Ensemble as its director (*Intendant*), Heli, whom father had originally met in the theater in Berlin, also took control of his literary legacy, and was determined to make the poems better known. When she died in 1971, my half sister and brother came to me, and though I was sick in bed, told me, "Barbara, you are not doing anything much, so please take care of Papa's work."

It seemed to all of us quite natural that I, like my mother, would be good in taking care of such things, although some people were furious that a woman could decide what could and could not be done with the plays. Despite the prominence of these plays, I've also devoted a great deal of time to getting all of Papa's poems in print, and would constantly ask my colleagues which poems had not yet been published, whether because of political or prudish caution (the love sonnets, for example, were left out of the original publication). Over time, the poems—which he deliberately wrote so clearly and simply that even the nodding donkey that he kept on his desk could understand—have multiplied, so much so that they now form, I'm proud to say, an important body of twentieth-century German poetry.

Translated here by David Constantine and Tom Kuhn,

Love Poems begins a major collaboration by these two gifted Oxford scholars to bring the vast body of Papa's poetry into English. Upon a lifetime of reflection, I have found that the poems will do different things to each who reads them, but most important, I want people to enjoy my father's poems and for them to be remembered.

—BARBARA BRECHT-SCHALL,
from an interview with Robert Weil,
Berlin, January 2014

TRANSLATORS' INTRODUCTION

T S. Eliot, writing on Tennyson, found in him "three qualities which are seldom found together except in the greatest poets: abun-dance, variety, and complete competence." Bertolt Brecht (1898–1956) is a great poet, one of the three or four best in the whole of German literature (a literature not short of first-rate poetry). He is abundant: the Berlin-Frankfurt edition of his complete works contains more than two thousand poems. He is various, on many topics, from shifting points of view, in all the registers. He is widely eclectic, a thieving magpie of much of world literature, he took from Greece and Rome, China, Japan, Britain, America, his own compatriots, the living and the long dead, across frontiers of space and time. His technical virtuosity in traditional forms and in forms he invented or developed for his own needs, is breathtaking. He works effectively in hexameters, in tight rhyming quatrains, sonnets, ballads, unrhyming verse in irregular meters and in numerous other shapes and forms as the poetic occasion demands. For any just assessment of his total poetic oeuvre we should have to consider his dramas, too: the tense, sometimes violent verse of *Saint Joan of the Stockyards*, *The Caucasian Chalk Circle*, and (out of Hölderlin's idiosyncratic translation) *Antigone*; the poignant lyricism of passages in *The Good Person of Szechwan*, the parodistic Shakespearian blank Verse of

Arturo Ui; the songs in many plays; and more, much more, besides. Brecht was a thorough poet. Throughout his writing life he thought constantly about the idea and the practice of poetry, about forms, about their nature, possibilities, best uses; and he adapted his thinking and his practice continually to answer the violently disrupting demands of the times and the places he lived in. This constant reflection on poetry, and the lifelong making of poetry, produced in Brecht a rare coherence of important things to say and of apt ways of saying them.

In the English-speaking world Brecht is still best known as a dramatist and theoretician on drama; and even his standing there is perhaps less than it should be since some in Britain and America—those who have not read his work, or not with an open mind—wrongly think of him as dogmatically bound into a politics which, so the "reasoning" goes, has no relevance since the walls came down. We will not argue against that wrong view here. But any doubters about Brecht might be helped into a closer understanding of him through the poetry. Poetry, by its very nature, resists being reduced to any dogmatic, let alone fundamentalist, view of the world. Poems may debate with an ideology but won't be bound by it. Brecht knew that; he knew very well what the peculiar resources and effects of poetry are. He knew that poetry can help in ways which are peculiarly its own.

Even in Germany, the true scope, variety, and force of Brecht's poetry did not begin to become apparent until after his death and the compiling of the complete editions of his work. And readers without German, after the three-volume Methuen translations published in 1976 and long out of print, have not been in a position to extend and refine their enjoyment and understanding of Brecht the poet. Our translations of a large selection of his poetry, already well advanced, will go some way, we hope, towards giving him his due in America and Britain and throughout the English-speaking world. Meanwhile this volume of love poems will be the forerunner and sign of the abundance to come.

Brecht, like Goethe, was a lyric poet all his writing life. He is known, very properly, for his engagement, as a writer, in the bitter and violent politics of his age, but he should also be known, quite as much as Goethe, as a poet driven by Eros. Like Goethe, Brecht was always more or less in love, and in his total oeuvre love, or let us say Eros, is expressed, discussed, enacted in an astonishing variety of modes, forms, tones, and circumstances. The first person singular in poetry—even in lyric poetry—can only very rarely be conflated with or confined to the person writing the poem. This is well known, but in Brecht's case it perhaps needs saying again and with some emphasis. In his poetry, no less than in his plays, he is a versatile inhabiter of roles: literary, historical, and biographical, as well as many others, male and female, that he fabricates and tries out in situations that interest him. He is a poet of many *personae*—which word comes from the Latin *personare*, meaning "to sound through," one sense of the word *persona* being the mask a Roman actor wore and spoke his lines through. The wearing of a mask, the adoption of a persona in poetry, far from serving evasiveness and mendacity, is an effective way of getting at the truth and making it evident. And that is the case with love poems as much as with any other sort.

Brecht's love poems, often intimately personal, are also rich in impersonal exemplars; that is, characters who in certain situations, employing certain kinds of discourse and strategies, illustrate possible human dealings in a variety of social contexts. Altogether Brecht led an "exemplary" life. The course and shape of it were to a great extent determined by events in his nation and in the world. For all his often vehemently asserted individuality, he led a life which was in large measure typical, and as a writer he drew attention to that typicalness. Born 1898, having served as a medical orderly in the First World War, he was a close witness of much of its aftermath: the November Revolution, Kapp Putsch, Hitler Putsch, hyperinflation, the increasingly violent polarization of politics during the later years of the Weimar Republic, the collapse of the markets in 1929. And in 1933, on the day after the Reichstag Fire, he went into exile, first in Scandinavia then in the United States. Postwar then, he was uneasily at home in the new GDR. During the uprising of June 1953 there was fighting on the Chausseestrasse, almost under his window. Some in the West (unfairly) thought him the exemplar of compromise. He died in 1956, a couple of months before the failed revolution in Hungary. Millions of people lived through or died in the events of that half century. Every one of those lives has its exemplary or figurative sense. Brecht had eyes to see that sense and in his writings he made it clear. He appears, very often in the third person, as an emblematic figure: the playwright, the teacher, the exile; or as a named personage: poor B.B., Me-Ti, Herr Keuner. And we can add "the lover" to those figures, the lover in times and circumstances and under a social order often very inimical to love and its free enjoyment and fulfilment. In the savagely disillusioned *Reader for City-Dwellers* love suffers as friendship and comradeship do; the times, the ideology of commodification and mercantile transaction, make it hard for lovers to prosper or even survive. See here the two poems from that collection (in a woman's voice): "He was easy to get . . ." and "Again and again . . ." And consider also, in the plays, Shen Te's love for the out-of-work pilot Sun, and the wistful erotic interest the Meat King and Philanthropist Mauler takes in Johanna, the young woman in whom he detects feelings he will not allow himself in the life he has chosen to lead.

The love poems are not a category apart. As already indicated, love, like all other human dealings, is affected by social circumstances. In the Augsburg Sonnets, for example, as in the *City-Dwellers* poems, Brecht acts out some of the worst possibilities. He presents himself, as the male protagonist, quite often in a singularly unattractive light. In part this is a young man's posturing; but posturing itself, understood as acting out, was an important poetic strategy throughout his career. So in poems of the early 1920s, acting cynically, he demonstrates a way of being human that is characteristic not just of a young man but of a young man in the big city between two wars. This important matter of the exemplary, of behavior which is figurative of the times and circumstances, will become clearer in our large edition of Brecht's poetry when we set the poems out abundantly through their successive phases, the successive social, political, and personal contexts in which they were produced.

Adjudicating a poetry competition in 1926, Brecht refused to award the prize to any of the more than five hundred entries. In none, he said, was there any successful attempt to communicate anything of any value to anybody. None of the poems was *of any use*. And lyric poetry especially, he declared, is something of which we must be allowed to ask "what use is it?" His own answers to that fair and important question were, in the course of his life, various, subtle and profound; but here we need only note that in love poetry, too, in Brecht's at least, usefulness (*Gebrauchswert*) is a constituent factor. In his sonnets, but not only there, Brecht as love-poet puts himself into the Renaissance and Baroque tradition of writing poems with a purpose, to persuade, to seduce. Or the poems give instructions—sardonic, brutal, or tender. Their *Gestus* is very often that of a person trying to make something happen. And in that stance, of course, they belong fully among the many poems Brecht wrote in the wish to induce people to think in a particular way, to arm themselves in the struggle against fascism.

More generally, Brecht's love poems almost always are what, in his view, none of the poems he adjudicated were: they are a communicative act, they address a person or persons in ways that require attention. Readers will very often have to adjust their thinking, their expectations, to attend to the communication, and perhaps to answer back. Something is in play, at stake, between Brecht (his poem) and the addressee, a dialogue is being offered, never an easy one. With Margarete Steffin and, to a lesser extent, with Ruth Berlau, Brecht entered into real poetic exchanges. A poem was sent and responded to, answered, a conversation, most often very testing and unsettling, was carried on in verse.

Steffin was Brecht's friend and lover for nearly ten years until she died of tuberculosis in Moscow in June 1941. She was also his closest collaborator in the literary work which he and she equally understood as an act of resistance to Hitler, in the cause of humanity. She was, as he himself said, his pupil, his teacher, his soldier, his general. Brecht has often been accused of using people, women especially; but his relationship with Steffin, his love for her and his work with her, should make us think more understandingly about what it meant, in those times, in that struggle, to use and to be used. Both equally desired, and thought it their responsibility, to be useful to the cause. Brecht's poems to Steffin, several of them in this volume, the rest to follow, are poems of a love which is, in its mixed entirety, tender, sensual, solicitous, jealous, protective, unkind, and kind. But at the heart of it, unchanging, was a loving and fighting collaboration, a commitment to serve, to use and to be used, in a matter which, quite rightly, they understood to be one of life or death. Seen like that, Brecht and Steffin, in that dialectic, using and being used, have considerable poignancy and nobility. They were engaged in unselfish action, in times which threatened to deform and deprave even the most usual and decent human dealings. Brecht, the lover and love-poet, is in that context an emblem of, at the very least, the desperate struggle to keep faith, hope, and love alive, and as such he, and his lover and comrade Steffin, deserve sympathy and admiration.

The organization of this volume is chronological (from 1918 to 1955) but with some slight shifts now and then for variety of tone, and also with groupings of poems addressed to or concerned with particular women. Brecht's love poems, so various in form, voice, register, feeling, and argument, belong entirely in the whole oeuvre to which they here give access.

—DAVID CONSTANTINE
and TOM KUHN

BERTOLT BRECHT
LOVE POEMS

BAAL'S SONG

If I find a well-stacked woman, then I take her in the hay,
Lift her skirts and let the breeze in, in the sun—for
  that's my way.

If she bites me *in flagrante*, then I wipe her down with hay,
Mouth and teeth and crotch, gallantly: nice and
  clean—for that's my way.

If the wench gets in a fever of excitement at our play,
I salute and laugh and leave her, friendlily—for that's
  my way.

O YOU CAN'T KNOW WHAT I SUFFER . . .

O you can't know what I suffer
When I see a woman who
Sways her yellow silk-clad bottom
Under skies of evening blue.

A BITTER LOVE SONG

Let things be now as they will
She was once very dear to me
So I know this also: once
She must have been very beautiful.

But now I no longer know how she looked then:
One day extinguished what for seven months shone.

HOWEVER THAT MAY BE, THERE WAS A TIME . . .

All the girls, I've long since forgotten them
Yet I remember they were once good to kiss
Just of her, only her, my most beloved
Not even this.

SONG OF LOVE

Side by side sat Heider Hei with Tine Tippe in the
    grass
The bright sun shone on them
And Hei asked Tine, No or yes?
And she laughed at him.
Oh how she laughed at him!

THE YOUTH AND THE MAIDEN

(Chastity ballad in a major key)

Oh they were melting into one!
He was feeling: she is mine.
And the darkness egged them on.
She was feeling: we're alone.
And he kissed her forehead for
She was not a bad girl nor
Did she want to cross that line.

Oh their hands' delicious playing!
Oh her heart went clippety-clop!
He is praying, she is praying
That he'll stir her courage up.
And she kissed his forehead for
She was not a bad girl nor
Knew what point or if to stop . . .

So as not to desecrate her
Now he visited a whore
Learned the festivals of Nature
And the art of spewing there.
Dipping in her body he

Washed away unchastity
Swore himself chaste ever more.

She however to put out
The guiltless fire he had lit
Attached herself to one without
Scruple who was fit for it.
He was rough, he laid her out
On the stairs, hard. And yet
Oh the grip of him was bliss!
She was not a nun and this
Stirred in her the taste for it.

And he praised his brain that had
Directed him the clever way
When he kissed her on the forehead
In the joyous month of May.
She the bad girl, he the dickhead
Branded on their brows they read:

It's a mucky game we play.

HALF IN MY SLEEP . . .

Half in my sleep in the pale beginning light
Against your body, many a night: that dream.
Ghostly highways under evening-pale
Very cold skies. Pale winds. Crows
Screaming for food and in the night comes rain.
With clouds in the wind, years following on years
Your face washes away, my Bittersweet, again
And in the cold wind with a shock of fear I feel
Your body lightly, half in my sleep, in the beginning
    light
Still with a trace of bitterness in my brain.

THE DAYS OF ALL YOUR BITTERNESSES . . .

The days of all your bitternesses
Will soon be over now, my dear
Like those òf our unheard-of kisses
Which all too soon have disappeared.

Soon life will give up all its substance
And death itself will lose its hurt
You'll take the line of least resistance
And sleep in peace in the hallowed dirt.

ON VITALITY

1

The main thing is vitality
A slug of brandy, and you're sorted
Any wench, law of causality
Must bend to vitality, even court it.

2

Women may lie in knots on your bed
Take your whip and not your morality!
Or do it outside, that's just as good
As long as you have vitality.

3

Vitality will always ease
Your path with any dumb angel. Vitality.
She'll see the Judgment and beg on her knees
For rites of bare legality.

4

Vitality can fully dispense
With soul or intellect

It's more concerned with a sixth sense
And women you can disrespect.

5

Vitality couldn't give a fig
For responsibility, consequences
Take Baal, for example, he was a pig
And a bundle of offences.

(So I pray to God, by night and day
For vi-tal-i-tay.)

THROUGH THE ROOM
THE WILD WIND COMES . . .

Through the room the wild wind comes
As the child ate purple plums
Then she offered her pale self
To the pleasures of the flesh.

Showed him tactfully how to take it
First insisting he go naked.
Apricots as sweet as these
Can't be fucked in dungarees.

And however wild our games were
Nothing was too much for her.
Afterwards she washed it nicely:
All just as it should by rights be.

DOWN IN THE WILLOW GROVE . . .

Down in the willow grove
Wind blowing wild
She, 'cause her mother called
Did it and smiled . . .

Wild the wind overhead
Clouds in the skies
She, 'cause it's dark by now
Kept shut her eyes.

And 'cause the grass is wet
Cold are the skies
She, on a willow stump
Gave up her prize.

When the new moon hangs red
In willows wild:
She will float down the stream:
Virgin and child.

THE SEVENTH PSALM

1

My beloveds, I know it: my hair is falling out with this wild living and I must lay me down on the stones. You see me drinking the cheapest schnapps and I go naked in the wind.

2

But, my beloveds, once upon a time I was pure.

3

I had a woman, she was stronger than me as the grass is stronger than the bull. The grass lifts up again.

4

She saw that I was bad and she loved me.

5

She did not ask where the way led that was her way and perhaps it led downward. When she gave me her body she said: That is all. And it became my body.

6

Now she is not anywhere anymore, she vanished like
the cloud when it has rained, I let her go and she fell,
for that was her way.

7

But at night sometimes when you see me drinking I
see her face white in the wind and strong and turned
my way, and I bow into the wind.

HEH. PSALM 9

1

Hear me, friends, I sing you the song of Heh, the dark-skinned, my beloved for sixteen months until her dissolution.

2

She did not grow old, she had undiscriminating hands, she sold her skin for a cup of tea and herself for a whip. She ran among the willows till she was tired, Heh!

3

She offered herself like a fruit but was not accepted. Many had her in their mouths and spat her out, the good woman, Heh. The beloved, Heh.

4

In her head she knew what a woman is but not with her knees. With her eyes in daylight she knew the way but in the dark she did not know it.

5

In the night she was wretched, blind with vanity, Heh, and women are nocturnal creatures and she was not.

6

She was not wise like Bi, the lovable, Bi, the plant, she ran hither and thither and her heart was unthinking.

7

And for that reason she died in the fifth month of year 20, a quick and secret death when nobody was looking and vanished like a cloud of which people say: it never was.

THE ELEVENTH PSALM

1

Evenings by the river in the dark heart of the bushes
sometimes I see her face again, hers, the woman I
loved, my woman, dead now.

2

It is many years ago and at times I know nothing
about her anymore who was once all things to me but
all things pass.

3

And she was in me like a small juniper on the
Mongolian steppes, concave with a washed-out yellow
sky and great sadness.

4

Our dwelling place was a black hut by the river. Often
and grievously the horseflies bit her white body. I read
the newspaper seven times, or I said: Your hair is the
colour of dirt. Or: You are heartless.

5

But one day when I was washing my shirt in the hut she walked to the gate and looked at me and wanted to go out.

6

And the man who had beaten her till he was tired said: My angel—

7

And the man who had said: I love you, led her out and looked up into the air with a smile and praised the weather and gave her his hand.

8

Then since she was outside in the air and it grew desolate in the hut he shut the gate and sat himself down behind the newspaper.

9

I haven't seen her since and all that remained of her was the little shout she gave when she came back to the gate in the morning and it was already shut.

Now the hut has rotted and my breast is stuffed with
newspaper and in the evenings I lie by the river in the
dark heart of the bushes and remember.

The wind has a grassy smell in its hair and the water
cries unceasingly to God for peace and I have a bitter
taste on my tongue.

12TH PSALM

1

I have eaten grass, yes I have, and taken my friend
Orge at his word, I swear, I have stolen, I don't deny it.
But I did not take her body, I couldn't.

2

I'm not a black, I don't say that out of modesty, but
I diligently carry out my duties. But our bodies lay
together between the sheets and I bit her in the throat
and fell asleep.

3

Because in her blood she had dark auto-da-fés,
lanterns and nigger dances and the weariness of many
highways: but I was a little idiot.

4

Fat animals crept through the brown boles of the
jungle around us, blue rain thundered in the plane-
tree roofs and we lay like gentle plants.

5

That was Heh, the dark-skinned, she died like a cloud
that has almost never been.

REMEMBERING MARIE A.

I

On that day in the blue month of September
Quietly under a young plum tree
I held her like a sweet dream in my arms
My pale love, and she was quiet with me.
And above us in the fair heavens of summer
There was a cloud, some while I saw it there
It was very white and high, so high, above
And when I looked again it was there no more.

2

Since that day many many moons have gone
Swimming quietly down, down and away
No doubt the plum trees have been felled by now
And if you ask, And what about love? I say
In answer I cannot now remember
But I do know what you mean, of course I do
But her face, in truth, I wouldn't know it now
I kissed it once upon a time, that's all I know.

3

And even the kiss I'd have long since forgotten
Had it not been that the cloud was also there

The cloud I do remember and always will
It was very white and high when it came over.
Who knows, perhaps the plum trees do still blossom
And that woman by now, perhaps, has seven children
But only a few minutes did that cloud blossom
And vanished in the wind when I looked up again.

THE RIVER
SINGS PRAISES . . .

The river sings praises. Stars in the trees.
The smell of thyme and peppermint.
Our brows are freshened by a little breeze
We are the children, this is God's present.
The grass is soft: the woman without bitterness
The lovely willows make everything rejoice:
Pleasure's a certainty for those who will say yes.
Never again would you want to leave this place.

To M

That night you didn't come I couldn't sleep but went
Many times to the door and it
Was raining and I went back in again.

I didn't know it then but I know it now:
That night it was already like the later nights
When you never came again and I couldn't sleep
And was already scarcely waiting anymore
But many times went to the door
Because it was raining there and cool.

But after those nights and still in later years
Whenever the rain dripped I would hear your
    footsteps
Outside the door and in the wind your voice
And your crying on the cold corner because
You couldn't get in.
For that reason I got up often in the night and
Went to the door and opened it and
Let in whoever had no home
And beggars came and whores, dossers
And all manner of folk.

Now many years have passed and even if
Rain still drips and the wind blows
If you came now in the night I know

I wouldn't know you anymore, not your voice
And not your face because things have changed.
Yet I still hear footsteps in the wind
And weeping in the rain and that somebody
Wants to come in.

And I've a mind to go to the door
And open it and see has no one come—
But I don't get up and I don't go out
Don't see
And nor does anybody come

ON THE WAY FROM AUGSBURG TO TIMBUKTU . . .

On the way from Augsburg to Timbuktu I met
    Marianne Zoff
Who sang in the opera and looked like a Maori
    woman
And was beautiful in the grass, in bed too and also in
    her clothes she looked beautiful
And I slept with her and got her pregnant.
(In her sleep she rolled up like a hedgehog.
She was cunning like an animal but her actions were
    without cunning
When she laughed she nodded her head, looked up at
    you aslant and pulled a blade of grass through her teeth
She walked for the joy of it
Once she said to me: Stoopid!
She was proud of her legs.
In her passion she had the appearance of scorched
    grass.)

BALAAM LAI IN HIS THIRTIETH YEAR...

Balaam Lai in his thirtieth year
Sailed one evening for Madagascar
Because of a longing to see Erna Susatte
Because it was four years since he'd
Seen her
And where she was he had no idea
And so he thought: She's in Madagascar.

He looked at the map in Thomas Cook. She'd
Very likely be there somewhere
He thought and so
He landed up in Madagascar
Rather
As Pontius Pilate did in the Creed.

He traveled with a case full of documents
An umbrella badly in need of splints
A guitar and a bottle of Johnnie Walker
And trouble in the heart, an old disorder.
But the sea is a damned bad-mannered critter
So he didn't give much thought to Erna Susatte
But once he was on the island then
The name (not the face) occurred to him again
But that night he went to bed alone, supposing
He'd hardly come across her the very first evening.

So when Balaam Lai in his thirtieth year
Suddenly one morning was in Madagascar
He asked himself before he went in search of her
Whether it was possible Erna Susatte
Was in Madagascar
And concluding it was possible, why shouldn't it be?
But that his chances of finding her were slight,
    especially
Since all he'd got with him was a suitcase and an
    umbrella
And since moreover the interest that he
Still had in the face of the vanished Erna Susatte
Was not great, not very great
And deciding over a vilely concocted punch
That Madagascar wasn't up to much
He sailed home moderately drunk on punch but
Shot of all the yearning and longing muck
And ordered another punch at The Red Carnation
12 Tauentzienstrasse, run
By another Erna, surnamed Clouds, this one.

Many years later, same street, number 4, in a bar
A supersaturated drunk used to relate
Among various true stories this one about
A daring trip in a schooner to Madagascar
Shipwreck, visions, snakebites
And a face he had seen deep in the swamps of
    Madagascar
As proof that now and then miracles do happen
For example when

With nothing to go on
He sees the pale and forgotten face of Erna Susatte
In an Asiatic
Swamp, drunk as a skunk on punch.

NOW IN THE NIGHT . . .

1

Now in the night while I love you
White clouds are in the silence in the sky
The waters make a roaring over stones
And the wind shivers in dead greenery.

2

White waters hurry
Down year after year
And in the sky there are
Clouds for evermore.

3

Later in the years of loneliness
Still there will be white clouds to see
And the waters will make a roaring over stones
And the wind will shiver in dead greenery.

NEED FOR ART

The virtuous woman who gives her lover all
And offers up herself to him quite freely
Must learn that good intentions are not really
Quite enough—he's also crying out for skill.

And even if her cry of "Iamyours"
Translates to sex with breakneck quickness
He isn't only interested in slickness
When it comes to emptying his swollen balls.

Although it may be love that stokes the fire
She'll need, for winters in these harsher years
Some real talent in that bum of hers.
More needful than a soulful gaze and sighs
(Although she'll need them too) are eager thighs
Performing tricks with gusto and desire.

THERE
AT THE BEGINNING . . .

There at the beginning, the first day
When that entwining couple entered here
The threshold knew they would not get away
It took the footfall that would be their last.
Behind the lattice the green tree sank to sere
And yellow discreetly, very fast
And climbing trembling to bed they were
With a smile by the wind they loved dismissed.

BALAAM LAI IN JULY

In July after the decline and fall of the Marquise
And his expulsion from Paradise
Standing in the dead bulrushes
At a pond with flies
Buzz buzz
Balaam Lai, supersaturated drunk that he was
Balaam Lai got smitten by the sun
God help us!
Balaam Lai, spirituous spirit of The White Carnation
Spat offhandedly into the pond of flies
Splash
Chewed things over and composed an invitation
To Anna Clouds
To join him that night in a solemn lamentation
And went and purchased another pair of duck eggs.
God have mercy on Anna Clouds!

But when the evening palely and in great pain began
    to darken
Balaam Lai had doubts
When Anna Clouds in the twilight came
Sailing along with her parasol, white as cream.
For Anna Clouds when it came to it was quite without
Any false delicacy in her free views
On love, God knows, she was the last person
To be fobbed off with lousy conjuring tricks

And not judge a man on his performance as though
He fed on the wafers of the Lord and raw eggs
And Balaam Lai knew this.
In brief, she observed that windows are made of glass
And when he didn't draw the curtains she did
And at eight o'clock was lounging on Balaam Lai's lily
  pad
(Whilst he like grim death read the *Evening News*).

Now when Anna Clouds began chewing her pink toes
  for boredom
Balaam Lai gave rapid thought as to how
This unchaste creature could be evicted from his
  wigwam
But saw no way and the best he could do
He thought, was trot off and buy red wine and quickly
  get
Her very drunk on it.

And she might pass out
While he sat over a noble and corpulent tome
  oppressed
By the decline and fall of the West.
But she, full of wine and wriggling around on his
  cushions,
Stared him stiff to share
What had occurred to her.
So then, she slugged the bottles and was the
  cold-soberest

Most frivolous person on earth when with all the
     winningness
Of a Valkyrie desperate for corpses
She invited him to join her in a little tenderness.

SONG OF LOST INNOCENCE FOLDING THE LINEN

1

The thing my mother told me
It can't be true, I'm sure.
She said, Once you are soiled
You'll never again be pure.
  That isn't true of the linen
  And it isn't true of me.
  Let the river run over the linen
  Quick it's clean as can be.

2

At eleven I was as sinful
As the cheapest girl-for-cash
And really not till fourteen
Did I mortify the flesh.
  A shade gray was the linen
  I dunked it, the river ran.
  Now it lies there fit for a virgin
  As though never breathed upon.

3

I was fallen already
Before I went with a man.
I stank to heaven, a scarlet
Whore of Babylon.

The linen in the river swishes
Gently to and fro
And feels in the rippling kisses:
How softly I whiten now.

4

For when my first embraced me
And I held him embraced
I felt from my breasts and belly
The wickedness released.

That's the way with linen
And that was the way with me.
The waters run, they hasten
Where the dirt cries, Set me free!

5

But when the others came
A doleful year began.
They gave me a bad name.
I was a bad woman.

Saving up and fasting
Was never a woman's cure.

Linen left long in the basket
Goes gray even there.

6

And then another followed
In another year.
I saw that myself and all things
Were other than before.
 Dip it in the river, rinse it!
 Sun, wind and dolly blue!
 Use it and dispense it:
 It will be good as new.

7

I know: much still may happen
Till nothing happens anymore.
But if you never wore it
What was the linen for?
 And when the linen's ragged
 And the dirt won't wash away
 The river takes the tatters.
 All comes to this one day.

BALLAD

And when she lay on her deathbed
She said to him: I have been
Faithful to you nearly fourteen years
And now what does it mean?

He spoke to her and held her hand
That was whiter than the sheets of the bed.
My dear wife, for these fourteen years
I thank you, he said.

The dress I always wore, she said
The color of it was gray
And what I ate was soup and fish
I'm almost sorry to say.

He held her hand the way someone holds
A weak rope in the sea
Already drowning and said: You were
A good wife to me.

And she said to him, How quickly it goes!
How white my hand is, look!
And she saw the words "Like a broken reed"
On a page in an old schoolbook.

But he stood by her and said to her
(And didn't immediately know
Whether what he said was right) and he said:
Perhaps it's all one now.

DISCOVERY ABOUT
A YOUNG WOMAN

A morning's parting, and about to go my way
A woman in the doorway, casually observed
And then I saw: one strand in her hair was gray
And found I could not bring myself to leave.

Mutely I reached out for her breast, and when
She asked me why—pointing at last night's bed—
I would not go, for that had been the plan
I looked at her straight in the eye and said:

Even just one more night, I want to stay
But you must use your time; for that's the worst
A woman on the threshold there like you

And let's be quicker with the things we say
We had not thought that you were so far through.
And then desire rose and choked my words.

BALLAD OF
THE FAITHLESS WOMEN

1

You want a woman, son, so you can say, "she's mine"
That's never going to happen here of course
Either you've got the big mouth of a swine
Or else you've got the penis of a horse
There's always women who'd kick up a fuss
Don't go for them: they're really not worth much.

2

Lie to her, no one's got a bigger prick
And when you sit together, son, be canny
Keep a firm grip on your axe, or else some dick
Will stick a pillow underneath her fanny.
There's women who'd resist, shout out and such
Don't go for them: they're really not worth much.

3

Stick a knife in the bedpost when you go to rest
And don't go out unless you really must
And if you do, then take her too, that's best
Or else some other bloke will grab her breast.

There's women who'll give way to any touch
Don't go for them: they're really not worth much.

    4

Don't use her too hard—it's no joke
Or else you'll sleep too deep, that can be bad
If you're too sleepy for a smoke
She may run off to someone else's pad.
There's women might respect your sleep, keep watch
Don't go for them: they're really not worth much.

THE SONG OF SURABAYA-JOHNNY

I

I was young, God, I was just sixteen
You came up from Burma in the night
And you said I should be your woman
You would always be treating me right.
I asked what you did for a living
And you said as you looked straight at me
You'd a job or something with the railroad
And you'd nothing to do with the sea.
You talked a lot, Johnny
A lot of lies, Johnny
From the very first day, Johnny, you were nothing
    but a cheat
I hate you so, Johnny
As you stand there grinning, Johnny
Take that pipe out of your mouth, you rat.
    Surabaya-Johnny, why must you be such a cad?
    Surabaya-Johnny, oh God and I love you so bad.
    Surabaya-Johnny, ah why should I be sad?
    You have no heart, Johnny, and I love you so bad.

At first it was always Sundays
If I just went along with it all
But it didn't last more than a fortnight
And the house of cards began to fall.
We were up and down through the Punjab
From the hills and right down to the sea:
When I look at myself in the mirror
I look like I'm forty-three.
It wasn't love, Johnny
You were after cash, Johnny
But it was just your lips, Johnny, I was staring at.
You wanted it all, Johnny
And I gave you more, Johnny
Take that pipe out of your mouth, you rat.
    Surabaya-Johnny, why must you be such a cad?
    Surabaya-Johnny, oh God and I love you so bad.
    Surabaya-Johnny, ah why should I be sad?
    You have no heart, Johnny, and I love you so bad.

3

I hadn't the wit to wonder
How you'd come by that particular name
But all along the coastline
You had a certain sort of fame.
So one morning in our tuppenny lodgings
I'll be listening to the crash of the sea
You'll be off with no explanations
And your boat will be down at the quay.

You have no heart, Johnny
You are nothing but a heel, Johnny
And now you're leaving, Johnny, and how about that!
But I love you still, Johnny
Like the very first day, Johnny
Take that pipe out of your mouth, you rat.
    Surabaya-Johnny, why must you be such a cad?
    Surabaya-Johnny, oh God and I love you so bad.
    Surabaya-Johnny, ah why should I be sad?
    You have no heart, Johnny, and I love you so bad.

THE GUEST

Nightfall, but there's much still she wants told
Quickly he spills out seven years, nigh on
And hears in the yard a chicken being killed
And knows the household only had that one

He will eat little of its flesh next day
Help yourself, she says. Still full, he answers her
Where were you yesterday before you came?—In
    safety
And where is it you've come from?—Town. Not far.

Then quickly he gets to his feet. Time flies!
Smiling he says to her: Farewell.—And you?
He hesitates, lets fall his hand, she sees
Dust on his shoes of streets she does not know.

HE WAS EASY TO GET ...

He was easy to get.
It was possible on the second evening.
I waited till the third (and knew
I was taking a risk).
Then he said, laughing: it's the bath salts
Not your hair.
But he was easy to get.

For a month I left him straight after making love.
Every third day I stayed away.
I never wrote.
But store up snow in a pot
It gets dirty all the same.
I did more than I could
When it was already over.

I threw out the bitches who were sleeping with him
As though I didn't mind
I did it laughing and crying.
I turned on the gas
Five minutes before he arrived, I
Borrowed money in his name:
It did no good.

But one night I slept
And one morning I got up

I washed myself from head to toe
Ate and said to myself:
That's it now.

Truth is:
I slept with him twice more
But by God and my mother
It was nothing.
Like everything else
It passed.

AGAIN AND AGAIN . . .

Again and again
When I look at this man
He hasn't been drinking and
He laughs as he used to
I think: things are getting better.
Spring is coming, good times are coming
The times that have gone
Have come again
Love is beginning again, soon
Things will be as they were.

Again and again
When I have been speaking to him
He has eaten and he does not go away
He talks to me, nor
Does he have his hat on
I think: it will be good
The ordinary time has passed—
You can talk to a person, he listens
Love is beginning again, soon
Things will be as they were.

The rain
Can't go back up

When the wound
No longer hurts
The scar does.

TERCETS ON LOVE—
THE LOVERS

See how those cranes fly arcing through the sky!
The clouds they have for company on their way
Were there already when they had to fly

From one life to another far away.
Together at the selfsame height and pace
It seems an almost casual display.

That crane and cloud just chance to share the space
Of the wide skies through which they pass so briefly
So neither one may linger in this place

And all they see is one another slightly
Rocking on the wind in loose accord
Who now in flight lie side by side so lightly

The wind may carry them off into the void.
If they remain themselves, and hold on tight
They can be touched by nothing untoward

It doesn't matter if they're driven out
Threatened by gunshots or by stormy weather.
Indifferent to the sun and moon's pale light

They journey on, besotted with each other.
What are you fleeing from?

    —The world.

        —Where to?

           —Wherever.

You ask how long now have they been together?

Not long.

    —And when they'll part?

        —Oh, soon enough.

So love appears secure to those who love.

SPRING

Spring is coming.
Between the sexes the game resumes
The lovers find their way to one another.
The beloved's gently enclosing hand
Shocks the girl's breast cold.
Her glance seduces him.

2

In a new light
The landscape appears to the lovers in spring.
The first flocks of birds are sighted
Very high.
The air is already warm.
The days are becoming long and the meadows
Keep their brightness late.

3

The growth of the trees and grasses in spring
Is measureless.
Fruitful unceasingly
Is the forest, are the meadows, the fields.
And the earth gives birth to the new
Without heed.

THE FIRST SONNET

When we were first divided into two
And one of our beds stood here and one stood there
We picked an inconspicuous word to bear
The sense we gave it: I am touching you.

The pleasure of such speaking may seem paltry
For touch itself is indispensable
But we at least kept "it" inviolable
And saved for later, like a surety.

Stayed ours, and yet removed from you and me
Could not be used yet had not ceased to be
Not rightly there and yet not gone away

And standing among strangers we could say
This word of ours as in the common tongue
And mean by it: we know where we belong.

THE THIRD SONNET

Already thinking we were of a mind
I used—and it was almost without knowing—
The words whose meaning was what we were doing
The commonest such words, the vulgarest kind.

All over again it shocked you through as though
Till now you had not seen what thing we did.
In many weeks of you with me in bed
Of words like that I scarcely taught you two.

But with such words I summon up the shock
Afresh of my first fleshly knowing you.
It can't be hidden any longer now
Of all your favors you kept not one back.

How could you make yourself common as muck?
The word for what it was you did was

EIGHTH SONNET

At night, by the hedge they hung the washing on . . .
By the stream in the wood, you were standing,
    wilderness . . .
In the small wooden bed, under the bronze likeness . . .
On a Swedish bed in the workroom just begun

Drying . . . On the hillside, at a steep angle . . .
Behind the cupboard by the window in the writing
    room . . .
At the inn, the oil stove stank . . . In that same
Storage corner of the writing room, postprandial . . .

Excited by pianos in the monastery . . .
Furnished; you threw the key down from the
    balcony . . .
In that hotel—in one room, in both rooms . . .

In the Motherland of the Proletariat . . . All times
Of day, all times of night . . . Occasions
In at least four countries and in all four seasons.

BUYING ORANGES

In a yellow fog along Southampton Street
Suddenly a barrow, a slattern plucking at
Her paper bags, and fruit in lamplight.
I stopped struck dumb like one who has seen what
He was running after: there put in his way.

Oranges! No thing else could it ever be!
I blew some warmth into my hands and quickly
Fished in my pockets after cash, to pay

But then between the pence being in my grip
And glancing at the price there written up
In smudged charcoal on newspaper
I caught my own wry whistling undertone
For at that moment bitterly this came clear:
Of course you are not anywhere in this town.

WHEN WE
HAD BEEN APART . . .

When we had been apart longer than ever before
Fearfully I searched your letters through for such
Words unknown to me as would say you were
No longer the one I know so well and miss so much.

And yet it must be that, seeing one another again
At once we'd recognize how in need we are

THE TWELFTH SONNET

On Dante's poems to Beatrice

And even now above her dusty tomb
Whom he was not allowed to fuck but stalked
With shuffling steps whatever ways she walked
The air we breathe still shivers at her name.

For he commanded us to think of her
And wrote such verses for her that indeed
We cannot help but heed them and concede
How beautiful his praises of her are.

Oh, the perniciousness that man inspired
By praising with such mighty praises what
He only ever looked at, never tried!

For since he sang her he had only eyed
What looks nice, crosses the street, is never wet
Counts as an object fit to be desired.

THE THIRTEENTH SONNET

The word you've often said I should not use
Comes from the Italian of Florence
From *fica*, meaning: *vulva*. They accuse
Even great Dante of vulgarity since
The word comes in his poems. Today I read
That for this he was vilified as once Paris was
Over Helen (though Paris, it must be said
Had more fun in his story than Dante did in his).

So even the sombre Dante as you see
Got caught up in the quarrels that arise
Around this thing that else earns only praise.
Not only Machiavelli teaches us:
In life and books much hot controversy
Has raged around this justly famous *locus*.

THOUGHTS OF A
STRIPPER DURING THE
ACT OF UNDRESSING

My lot it is—the world is such a mess—
To serve as handmaid unto art, my task:
Vouchsafe these gents a little happiness
Yet if you ask

Precisely what I feel as I unwrap
Myself and decorously prance about
Under the golden lamps, doing the strip
I'll answer: nowt.

I'm sure to miss my bus. It's nearly twelve.
The cheese is better in the old arcade.
The fat girl says she's gonna drown herself.
He's got a blade.

Half-empty. Saturday! It'll be late tonight.
I'd better smile. The air in here's a stench
Shut up you hounds, you'll see 'em soon, all right?
But what about the rent . . . ?

And now I haven't stopped the milk, not good.
Do I have to show my bum as well? Well quick
I'll wiggle it a bit, that's all. The food
In the Yellow Dog's enough to make you sick.

NANNA'S SONG

1

There I was, just seventeen,
Selling love out on the streets.
Isn't much I haven't seen:
Pretty nasty stuff
When the going's tough—
Fit to turn you off the game for keeps.
(After all, I'm not an animal, you know.)
    Just thank Christ the whole thing's quickly over
    All the loving, the worry and fear.
    Where are the tears that flowed so freely?
    Where are the snows of yesteryear?

2

With the years there's no mistaking
It gets easier to do—
Up the numbers you are taking:
It's no life of ease
Your emotions freeze
If you never grant them what they're due.
(After all, stocks won't last for ever.)
    Just thank Christ the whole thing's quickly over
    All the loving, the worry and fear.

Where are the tears that flowed so freely?
Where are the snows of yesteryear?

3

Even if you learn quite quickly
How to sell yourself and smile
Selling sex for cash is strictly
Not a lot of fun,
But you get it done
Though you're getting older all the while.
(After all, you can't be seventeen forever.)
    Just thank Christ the whole thing's quickly over
    All the loving, the worry and fear.
    Where are the tears that flowed so freely?
    Where are the snows of yesteryear?

THE MADAM'S SONG

Oh, you know how people say a red moon
Shining on the water makes the girls go weak
And you've heard how all the ladies swoon
For a handsome bloke. Believe me, it's a joke!
   I've seen girls with hearts on fire
   But their thoughts were on—something higher.
   Though it may not seem polite:
   Decent girls will quickly tire
   Of a gentleman who's tight,
   Yet they can be quite adoring
   If you learn to treat them right.
   Money makes a girl feel sexy—
   It's as true as it is trite.

So tell me, what's the use of a red moon
Shining on the water, if you're stony broke?
Handsome men don't have a silver lining:
When they're out of cash, believe me it's no joke.
   I've seen girls with hearts on fire
   But their thoughts were on—something higher.
   Though it may not seem polite:
   Don't imagine you'll inspire
   All that passion and delight
   Till the girl has had her breakfast.

No my friend, that's just not right.
Food is good, and money's sexy—
It's as true as it is trite.

SONG OF
THE WIDOW IN LOVE

Oh I know I never should admit
That I tremble when he touches me
Oh however did I get like this
That I pray he'll lead me where he wants to be.
Sin's a thing wild horses wouldn't drag me to
If I didn't want him the way I do.

When I fought against love like I did
Let's be honest it was because without a doubt
Once I stand before him half-naked
He will strip me, he will clean me out.
Will he care when I reproach him? No.
If only I didn't want him the way I do.

I'm not sure that he is worthy of me
And is it really love he feels and when
He has gobbled up my savings won't he
Chuck the leavings of me in the bin?
Oh I know why I've told him no till now:
If only I didn't want him the way I do.

If I'd had a pennyworth of sense
I'd never have given him what (alas) he begged me for
I'd have slapped him round the head at once

If he—which he did—came too close and went too far
I wish he'd clear off where I told him to!
(If only I didn't want him the way I do.)

THE ACTRESS IN EXILE

(to Helene Weigel)

Now she puts on her makeup. In the white cell
She sits bowed on the simple stool
With light movements
She applies the makeup in the mirror.
Carefully she washes away from her face
All that is particular: the gentlest sensation
Will transform it. From time to time
She lets her frail and noble shoulders
Fall forward, like those who have to
Work hard. She already has on the rough blouse
With patches at the sleeves. The bast shoes
Stand on the makeup table.
When she's ready
She asks eagerly if the drum has arrived
On which the thunder of guns will be made, and
    whether the great net
Is in place. Then she stands, a small figure
Great warrior
To put on the bast shoes and represent
The struggle of the Andalusian fisherman's wife
Against the generals.

WHEN I'D REPORTED TO THE COUPLE, THUS . . .

*The Augsburger walks with Dante through the
hell of the departed. He addresses the inconsolable
and reports to them that on earth some things
have changed.*

When I'd reported to the couple, thus
That up there no one murders now for gain
Since no one owns a thing, the faithless spouse

Who'd beguiled that woman so improperly
Lifted his hand, now tied to hers by chains
And looked at her and turned perplexed to me

So no one steals, if there's no property?
I shook my head. And as their hands just touched
I saw a blush suffuse the woman's cheeks.

He saw it too and cried, She hasn't once
Shown so much since the day she was seduced!
And murmuring, Then there's no abstinence?

They moved off swiftly. And the ties that fused
Them tight were of no weight or consequence.

I SHALL GO WITH
THE ONE I LOVE . . .

I shall go with the one I love.
I shall not reckon what it costs.
I shan't consider if it's right.
I shall not ask if he loves me.
I shall go with him I love.

TO BE READ MORNINGS AND EVENINGS

He whom I love
Has told me
That he needs me.

That's why
I take care of myself
Watch my step and
Fear every raindrop
Lest it strike me down.

KIN-JEH SAID OF HIS SISTER

We loved one another between the battles.
From column to column
Marching by, we waved. There were letters
Poste restante in the taken cities. Awaiting my
    enemies
In hiding poorly housed
I heard her light tread, she
Brought food and news. Quickly at the railway station
We agreed how we should continue our operations.
With the dust of the road still on my lips
I kissed her. Around us
Everything changed. Our affections
Did not change.

OUR UNCEASING
CONVERSATION . . .

Our unceasing conversation that was like
The conversation of two poplars and that had lasted
    many years
Has fallen silent. I no longer hear
The things you say or write nor do you hear
The things I say.
I held you on my lap and combed your hair
I instructed you in the art of war
And taught you how to conduct yourself with a man
How to read books and how to read faces
How to fight and how to rest
But now I see
How much I never said to you.
Often I wake in the night choking
On useless counsels.

KIN-JEH'S SECOND POEM ABOUT HIS SISTER

Through all the years when after long absences
I entered her house I seemed expected and the chair
Set ready and the kettle on the hob.
Laughing she told me of all the stupidities
That had occurred. Hers included
And even mine. And I was always expecting
Her light step to my door, ready
To lay all else aside when she came in. Our
    experiences
We recounted like historical events, we spoke
Of the eight nights and the return from Spain
The trip in the Ford
And bringing the rug with us.

FRUITLESS CALL

O faint sea-roaring in the black receiver!
No rapid heartbeat, only an empty tick!
And then a whispering, as of seven towns, comes over
And a tired voice says: *svarer ikke.*

And so the faraway room must be empty.
You are not here. And now you are not there.
As though I heard: the ship must be at sea
And quite beyond any call from any quarter.

Our dialogue that had not needed voices
(For we could hear in things that went unsaid
The questions, new ones, rising nonetheless)
Our dialogue has only now gone dead.

19TH SONNET

Encounter with the ivory guardians

One day when no news of you had come
I summoned the guardians, the six elephants,
To the Arc de Triomphe and they took up their stance
That night towards eleven on the Avenue de Wagram.

They eyed me, swaying slightly. I said to them:
When I left her in your protection
I ordered you to trample anyone
She made complaint about to strawberry jam.

They stood in silence till the largest beast
Lifting his trunk, malignly slowly
Pointed, trumpeting, to the guilty party: me.

Like thunder all six charged. I fled. So chased
To the post office and squinting frightened through
The window I wrote the letter I owed you.

THE GOOD COMRADE M.S.

I came to you as a teacher and as a teacher
I might have departed from you. But because I learned
I stayed. For later also
Finding refuge beneath the Danish thatch
Even then I did not leave you.
And you gave me one from among you
To go with me.

So that she will test and check
Everything I say; and from now on
Correct every line
Being schooled in the school of the combatants
Against oppression.

Since then, in frail health but
Cheerful in the spirit
She has strengthened me. Not corruptible
Even by me. Often
With a smile I cross out a line myself already guessing
What she would say about it.

But in other company she defends me
I have heard she got up from her sickbed
To explain the usefulness of the *Lehrstücke* to you
Knowing as she does that I exert myself
To serve your cause.

THE 21ST SONNET

Hesitant, lifting the black receiver, so
Much fear was in me I had no delight
In the word *cured*. It was not till night
I vowed I'd send you a dream and a *laudatio*.

This is the dream: when you step into the daylight
Our guardian beasts shall bow their heads to you
And raise them trumpeting the respect you're due
For such conspicuous valour in a mortal fight.

Praised be whoever won't cast down the burden
That she was charged with though the ground give
     under her!
The greatest victory: the one that seemed beyond her!

The smallest whitest beast shall give you thanks for this
That you by courage and by canniness
Saved us the fighter and the good woman.

SONNET

And now it's war and now our way is tougher.
You fellow-wayfarer, my given comrade
On level ways or steep, narrow or wide
Teacher and taught, both being both together

And both in flight now with a common goal
Know what *I* know: that this goal's not more
Than the way itself, so should one of us fall
And the other let her, let him, only setting store

On the goal itself, the goal would disappear
Become unrecognizable, nowhere known
And breathless at the end the one arriving there
Would stand in sweat and a gray nothingness.
Here where we are now at this milestone
I ask the poem's muse to tell you this.

SONNET NO. 19

One thing I do not want: you flee from me.
Complain, I'll want to hear you anyway.
For were you deaf I should need what you say
And were you dumb I should need what you see

And blind: I'd want to see you nonetheless.
Given to watch for me, companion
The way is long and we're not halfway done
Consider where we are still: in darkness.

"Leave me, I'm wounded" is not good enough
And nor is "Somewhere," only "Here" will do.
Take longer with the task: but you can't be let off.

You know, whoever's needed is not free.
But come whatever may, I do need you.
I saying I could just as well say we.

THEN AT THE LAST, WHEN DEATH . . .

Then at the last, when death, who is not implacable
Showed me the four ruined lobes of her lungs and
    shrugged
And could not ask it of her that she live on the fifth
    alone
Speedily I assembled another five hundred tasks
Things to be dealt with at once, next day, next year
In the next seven years
Asked countless questions, critical questions, only
Answerable by her and so in demand
She died more easily.

WRECKAGE

There's the wooden box still for the notes when a play
    is being constructed
There are the Bavarian knives, the lectern is still there
There is the blackboard, there are the wooden masks
There's the little radio and the army trunk
There is the answer, but nobody asking the questions
High above the garden
Stands the Constellation of Steffin

REMEMBERING
MY LITTLE TEACHER . . .

Remembering my little teacher
Her eyes, the blue angry fire
And her worn cloak with the wide hood
And the wide hem, I named
Orion in the sky the Constellation of Steffin.
Looking up and contemplating it, shaking my head
I believe I hear a faint coughing.

IN THE NINTH YEAR
FLEEING FROM HITLER ...

In the ninth year fleeing from Hitler
Exhausted by the journeys
The cold and the hunger of Finland in winter
And waiting for the passport to another continent
Our comrade Steffin died
In the red city of Moscow.

MY GENERAL
HAS FALLEN . . .

My general has fallen
My soldier has fallen

My pupil has gone away
My teacher has gone away

The one who looked after me has gone
The one I looked after has gone

AFTER THE DEATH OF
MY COLLABORATOR M.S.

Since you died, little teacher
I go around not seeing, restless
In a gray world amazed
Without employment like a man dismissed.

I am denied
Admission to the workplace
Like any other stranger.

I see the streets and the public gardens
Now at unaccustomed times of the day and so
Scarcely recognize them.

Home
I cannot go: I am ashamed
That I am dismissed and in
Unhappiness.

WHEN I CAME BACK
FROM SAINT-NAZAIRE . . .

When I came back from Saint-Nazaire
I had no knickers on.
Oh, what a fuss there was at once:
Where have your knickers gone?
I said, Just outside Saint-Nazaire
The sky's too blue, too blue
And the oats stand tall, too tall
And the sky, the sky is too blue.

INSTRUCTION IN LOVE

Hearken, girl, to my advice
Try to make your cries endearing
I like souls to have some flesh
And flesh with soul is more alluring.

Chastity won't dampen lust
When I'm hungry I could eat you.
Virtue's better with a bust
And a bust in turn needs virtue.

Leda once was raped by Zeus
Now maidens fear to play along
Though she herself quite liked abuse:
The god would have his swanny song.

THE SONG OF FRATERNIZATION

Just seventeen I was
When the enemy came to town.
He offered me his arm
And laid his saber down.
 And after evensong
 Came May nights warm and long
 The regiment formed a square
 The bugle sounded, they stood at ease
 Then the enemy took us into the trees
 And fraternized, right there.

The enemy were many
My enemy was a cook
I hated him by day
At night I loved the schnook.
 For after evensong
 Come May nights warm and long
 The regiment forms its square
 The bugle sounds, they stand at ease
 Then the enemy takes us into the trees
 And we fraternize, right there.

The love that so consumed me
Was truly a force from above.
My folks could never grasp

That I didn't hate, just love.
One dank and dismal dawn
It turned to hurt and pain
The regiment formed the square
The bugle called, and with one accord
The enemy, and the man I adored
Marched off without a care.

THE PLUM SONG

That year as the plums were turning
From the north a horse and wain
Came to town one early morning
Driven by a fine young man.

As we gathered in the harvest
The stranger laid aside his hat
Stretched himself out in the meadow
Fell to watching this and that.

As we stewed the plums that summer
He was generous with his fun
Smiling stuck his purpled finger
In our saucepans one by one.

As we sat us down to eat them
He was long since up and gone
But, believe us, we could never
Quite forget that fine young man.

SAUNA AND SEX

Fuck first, then bathe—that's what I advise.
You wait till she bends down to take the bucket
Admire her naked arse before you fuck it
Then take her playfully between the thighs.

At first you have to hold her in position
Then she'll sit on top and rub her quim
Along your cock until her juices swim.
But then, and in accordance with tradition
She'll wait on you. She pours the boiling water
In generous splashes on the fizzing stones
She whips you sore with slender birch-tree switches
Till in the scalding steam your body twitches
And you refresh yourself just as you ought to
And sweat out all that fucking from your bones.

WEAKNESSES

You had none
I had one:
I loved.

WHEN I LEFT YOU, AFTERWARDS . . .

When I left you, afterwards
On that great today
I saw nothing, when I began
To see, but gaiety.

Since that evening, that hour
You know the one I mean
Livelier is my stride and more
Beautiful this mouth of mine.

Greener are, now that I feel,
Meadow, bush and tree,
The water is more lovely cool
That I pour over me.

MY LOVE GAVE ME
A LITTLE BRANCH . . .

My love gave me a little branch
With yellow leaves on.
The year goes to its end
Love has just begun.

SEVEN ROSES
THE ROSEBUSH HAS . . .

Seven roses the rosebush has
Six belong to the wind
But one remains so that I'll have
One rose to find.

Seven times I'll call your name
Six times stay away
But promise me the seventh time
You'll come right away.

WHEN IT IS FUN
WITH YOU . . .

When it is fun with you
Sometimes I think then
If I could die now
I'd have been happy
Right to the end.

When you are old then
And you think of me
I'll look like now
And you'll love a woman
Who is still young.

SMOKE

The little house among trees by the lake
From the roof smoke rises
If that weren't there
How cheerless they'd be
House, lake and trees.

LOVE SONG FROM
A BAD TIME

We were not friends to one another then
And yet for love it did not seem too soon
And so we lay there in each other's arms
Stranger to each other than the moon.

We'd likely fight about the price of fish
If we should meet at a marketstall today
We were not friends to one another then
Although in one another's arms we lay.

SEND ME A LEAF ...

Send me a leaf, but from a little tree
That grows no nearer your house
Than half an hour away. For then
You will have to walk, you will get strong and I
Shall thank you for the pretty leaf.

WHEN I HAVE TO LEAVE YOU DEAR …

When I have to leave you dear
For all the horses, men and gear
The queen's great ship will lie there waiting at the
quay.
Take another sweetheart, Minnie
For our ship goes to Virginny
And our love, our love my dear can never be.

And we'll stand there thousands strong
Wave you off with hurrah and song
As the queen's great ship sets sail for far-off lands.
Remember, Jimmy, as I kiss you
I will always always miss you
When I one day take another man.

NOTES

These notes provide, for every poem: the original German title; the volume and page reference to the standard German edition (the *Große kommentierte Berliner und Frankfurter Ausgabe*—*BFA*) on which our versions are, for the most part, based; the date or approximate date of composition; the date of first publication (indicated by P) insofar as we have been able to ascertain that (for poems first published after Brecht's death we have not always gone beyond the principal Suhrkamp Verlag publications); and the initials of the translator.

Baal's song   [Baals Lied]
BFA 11, 9; 1918; P1966, 1982 in this version; T.K.
Copyright © 1966, 1982 by Bertolt-Brecht-Erben / Suhrkamp Verlag

O you can't know what I suffer . . .   [O du ahnst nicht, was ich
                                              leide . . .]
BFA 13, 109; 1917/18; P1982; T.K.
Copyright © 1982 by Bertolt-Brecht-Erben / Suhrkamp Verlag

A bitter love song   [Ein bitteres Liebeslied]
BFA 11, 11; 1918; P1965; D.C.
This poem survives only as a fragment.
Copyright © 1965 by Bertolt-Brecht-Erben / Suhrkamp Verlag

However that may be,   [Wie dem auch sei,
there was a time . . .   einmal . . .]
BFA 13, 126; 1918; P1963; T.K.
This is possibly a sketch for a continuation of the previous poem.
Copyright © 1963 by Bertolt-Brecht-Erben / Suhrkamp Verlag

Song of love   [Lied von Liebe]
BFA 11, 12; 1918; P1975; D.C.
Copyright © 1975 by Bertolt-Brecht-Erben / Suhrkamp Verlag

The youth and the maiden   [Der Jüngling und die
                                              Jungfrau]
BFA 11, 13; 1918; P1961; D.C.
Copyright © 1961 by Bertolt-Brecht-Erben / Suhrkamp Verlag

Half in my sleep . . .   [So halb im Schlaf . . .]
BFA 13, 133; 1919; P1982; D.C.
Copyright © 1982 by Bertolt-Brecht-Erben / Suhrkamp Verlag

The days of all your bitternesses . . .   [Die Tage deiner
                                              Bitternisse . . .]
BFA 13, 132; 1919; P1963; T.K.
Copyright © 1963 by Bertolt-Brecht-Erben / Suhrkamp Verlag

On vitality   [Über die Vitalität]
BFA 13, 150; 1920; P1982; T.K.
Copyright © 1982 by Bertolt-Brecht-Erben / Suhrkamp Verlag

Through the room the wild   [Durch die Kammer
wind comes . . .   ging der Wind . . .]
BFA 13, 151; 1920; P1920 first stanza, 1982; T.K.
Copyright © 1982 by Bertolt-Brecht-Erben / Suhrkamp Verlag

Down in the willow grove . . .   [Dunkel im
                                              Weidengrund . . .]
BFA 13, 152; 1920; P1982; T.K.
Copyright © 1982 by Bertolt-Brecht-Erben / Suhrkamp Verlag

The seventh psalm [Der siebente Psalm:
Ich weiss es,
Geliebte . . .]

BFA 11, 20; 1920; P1960; D.C.

Copyright © 1960 by Bertolt-Brecht-Erben / Suhrkamp Verlag

Heh. Psalm 9 [Von He. 9. Psalm]

BFA 11, 22; 1920; P1965; D.C.

Copyright © 1965 by Bertolt-Brecht-Erben / Suhrkamp Verlag

The eleventh psalm [Der elfte Psalm: Abends
am Fluss . . .]

BFA 11, 23; 1920; P1960; D.C.

Copyright © 1960 by Bertolt-Brecht-Erben / Suhrkamp Verlag

12th psalm [12. Psalm]

BFA 11, 25; 1920; P1988; D.C.

There is a small gap in Brecht's text at the beginning of this poem,
implying a direct object for "stolen."

Copyright © 1988 by Bertolt-Brecht-Erben / Suhrkamp Verlag

Remembering Marie A. [Erinnerung an die Marie A.]

BFA 11, 92; 1920; P1924; D.C.

Copyright © 1924 by Bertolt-Brecht-Erben / Suhrkamp Verlag

The river sings praises . . . [Der Fluss lobsingt . . .]

BFA 13, 163; 1920; P1976; D.C.

Copyright © 1976 by Bertolt-Brecht-Erben / Suhrkamp Verlag

To M [An M]

BFA 13, 205; 1921; P1982; D.C.

Copyright © 1982 by Bertolt-Brecht-Erben / Suhrkamp Verlag

On the way from Augsburg [Auf dem Wege von
to Timbuktu . . . Augsburg . . .]

BFA 13, 206; 1921; P1993; D.C.

Copyright © 1993 by Bertolt-Brecht-Erben / Suhrkamp Verlag

Balaam Lai in his thirtieth year . . .   [Balaam Lai in seinem
                                          dreissigsten Jahr . . .]
BFA 13, 212; 1921; P1982; D.C.
Copyright © 1982 by Bertolt-Brecht-Erben / Suhrkamp Verlag

Now in the night . . .   [Jetzt in der Nacht . . .]
BFA 13, 216; 1921; P1960; D.C.
Copyright © 1960 by Bertolt-Brecht-Erben / Suhrkamp Verlag

Need for art   [Forderung nach Kunst]
BFA 13, 312; c.1925; P1982; T.K.
Copyright © 1982 by Bertolt-Brecht-Erben / Suhrkamp Verlag

There at the beginning . . .   [Am ersten Tage schon
                                gleich zu Beginne . . .]
BFA 13, 217; 1921; P1993; D.C.
Copyright © 1993 by Bertolt-Brecht-Erben / Suhrkamp Verlag

Balaam Lai in July   [Balaam Lai im Juli]
BFA 13, 231; 1921; P1982; D.C.
Copyright © 1982 by Bertolt-Brecht-Erben / Suhrkamp Verlag

Song of lost innocence   [Lied der verderbten
folding the linen   Unschuld beim
                           Wäschefalten]
BFA 13, 233; 1921; P1951; D.C.
Copyright © 1951 by Bertolt-Brecht-Erben / Suhrkamp Verlag

Ballad   [Ballade: Und als sie lag
           auf dem Sterbebett . . .]
BFA 13, 244; 1922; P1965; D.C.
Copyright © 1965 by Bertolt-Brecht-Erben / Suhrkamp Verlag

Discovery about a young woman   [Entdeckung an einer jun-
                                 gen Frau]
BFA 13, 312; c.1925; P1960; T.K.
Copyright © 1960 by Bertolt-Brecht-Erben / Suhrkamp Verlag

Ballad of the faithless women   [Ballade von
                                                  den untreuen
                                                  Weibern]

BFA 13, 330; 1926; P1982; T.K.
Copyright © 1982 by Bertolt-Brecht-Erben / Suhrkamp Verlag

The song of Surabaya-Johnny   [Surabaya-Johnny]
BFA 13, 344; 1926; P1929; T.K.
This song found its way into the play *Happy End*, by Brecht and
Elisabeth Hauptmann. It became a hit in the setting by Kurt Weill,
memorably sung by Lotte Lenya.
Copyright © 1929 by Bertolt-Brecht-Erben / Suhrkamp Verlag

The guest   [Der Gast]
BFA 13, 353; c. 1926; P1960; D.C.
This version includes a manuscript variant of the last two lines.
Copyright © 1960 by Bertolt-Brecht-Erben / Suhrkamp Verlag

He was easy to get . . .   [Es war leicht,
                                                  ihn zu bekommen . . .]

BFA 11, 170; 1926/27; P1960; D.C.
This and the next are taken from the short collection *Reader for
City-Dwellers.*
Copyright © 1960 by Bertolt-Brecht-Erben / Suhrkamp Verlag

Again and again . . .   [Immer wieder . . .]
BFA 11, 171; 1926/27; P1960; D.C.
Copyright © 1960 by Bertolt-Brecht-Erben / Suhrkamp Verlag

Tercets on love—The lovers   [Terzinen über
                                                  die Liebe—Die
                                                  Liebenden]

BFA 14, 15; 1928; P1930; T.K.
This poem also features as a dialogue, in more or less alternate
lines, between Jenny and Paul in *Rise and Fall of the City of
Mahagonny.*
Copyright © 1930 by Bertolt-Brecht-Erben / Suhrkamp Verlag

Spring   [Das Frühjahr kommt . . .]
BFA 14, 127; 1931; P1932; D.C.
Copyright © 1932 by Bertolt-Brecht-Erben / Suhrkamp Verlag

The first sonnet   [Das erste Sonett]
BFA 11, 185; 1932/33; P1964; D.C.
This and the next six poems are addressed to or have to do with
Margarete Steffin.
Copyright © 1964 by Bertolt-Brecht-Erben / Suhrkamp Verlag

The third sonnet   [Das dritte Sonett]
BFA 11, 186; 1933; P1988; D.C.
Copyright © 1988 by Bertolt-Brecht-Erben / Suhrkamp Verlag

Eighth sonnet   [Achtes Sonett: Nachts, wo
                                          die Wäsche . . .]
BFA 11, 191; 1933; P1982; D.C.
Copyright © 1982 by Bertolt-Brecht-Erben / Suhrkamp Verlag

Buying oranges   [Der Orangenkauf]
BFA 11, 195; 1934; P1964; D.C.
Copyright © 1964 by Bertolt-Brecht-Erben / Suhrkamp Verlag

When we had been apart . . .   [Als wir so lang getrennt . . .]
BFA 14, 332; 1936; P1965; D.C.
This poem survives only as a fragment.
Copyright © 1965 by Bertolt-Brecht-Erben / Suhrkamp Verlag

The twelfth sonnet   [Das zwölfte Sonett (Über
                                          die Gedichte des Dante
                                          auf die Beatrice)]
BFA 11, 190; 1934; P1938; D.C.
Copyright © 1938 by Bertolt-Brecht-Erben / Suhrkamp Verlag

The thirteenth sonnet   [Das dreizehnte Sonett]
BFA 11, 190; 1934; P1938; D.C.
Copyright © 1938 by Bertolt-Brecht-Erben / Suhrkamp Verlag

Thoughts of a stripper during   [Gedanken eines
the act of undressing   Revuemädchens]
BFA 14, 295; 1935; P1964; T.K.

Nanna's Song   [Nannas Lied]
BFA 14, 334; 1936; P1938; T.K.
This and the next are songs sung by characters in the play *Round Heads and Pointed Heads*, for which they were set to music by Hanns Eisler.

The madam's song   [Kuppellied]
BFA 14, 333; 1936; P1938; T.K.

Song of the widow in love   [Lied der liebenden
     Witwe]
BFA 14, 328; 1936; P1965; D.C.

The actress in exile   [Die Schauspielerin
     im Exil]
BFA 14, 355; 1937; P1937; T.K.
Helene Weigel played the title role at the première of *Señora Carrar's Rifles* in Paris in 1937.

When I'd reported   [Als ich den beiden so
to the couple, thus . . .   berichtet . . .]
BFA 14, 417; c.1938; P1964; T.K.

I shall go with the one I love . . .   [Ich will mit dem
     gehen . . .]
BFA 14, 458; c.1939; P1953; T.K.

To be read mornings and evenings   [Morgens und abends
                                     zu lesen]

BFA 14, 353; 1937; P1964; T.K.
This and the next four are addressed to or have to do with Ruth
Berlau.
Copyright © 1964 by Bertolt-Brecht-Erben / Suhrkamp Verlag

Kin-Jeh said of his sister   [Kin-Jeh sagte von
                              seiner Schwester]

BFA 14, 352; 1937; P1965; D.C.
Copyright © 1965 by Bertolt-Brecht-Erben / Suhrkamp Verlag

Our unceasing conversation . . .   [Unser unaufhörliches
                                     Gespräch . . .]

BFA 14, 354; 1937; P1965; D.C.
Copyright © 1965 by Bertolt-Brecht-Erben / Suhrkamp Verlag

Kin-Jeh's second poem   [Zweites Gedicht
about his sister   Kin-Jehs über
                              seine Schwester]

BFA 14, 356; 1937; P1965; D.C.
Copyright © 1965 by Bertolt-Brecht-Erben / Suhrkamp Verlag

Fruitless call   [Vergeblicher Anruf]
BFA 14, 430; 1939; P1982; D.C.
    svarer ikke—(Danish) "there's no reply."
Copyright © 1982 by Bertolt-Brecht-Erben / Suhrkamp Verlag

19th Sonnet   [19. Sonett. Begegnung
                              mit den elfenbeinernen
                              Wächtern]

BFA 14, 354; 1937; P1964; D.C.
This and the next ten all concern Margarete Steffin, who, having
followed Brecht into antifascist exile, died of tuberculosis in Moscow
in 1941.
Copyright © 1964 by Bertolt-Brecht-Erben / Suhrkamp Verlag

The good comrade M.S.   [Die gute Genossin M.S.]
BFA 14, 357; 1937; P1964; D.C.
Brecht used the term *Lehrstücke* for a loose group of plays from around 1930.
It is variously translated into English as "teaching plays" or "learning plays."
Copyright © 1964 by Bertolt-Brecht-Erben / Suhrkamp Verlag

The 21st sonnet   [Das 21. Sonett]
BFA 14, 418; c.1938; P1964; D.C.
Copyright © 1964 by Bertolt-Brecht-Erben / Suhrkamp Verlag

Sonnet   [Sonett: Und nun
           ist Krieg . . .]
BFA 14, 437; 1939; P1964; D.C.
Copyright © 1964 by Bertolt-Brecht-Erben / Suhrkamp Verlag

Sonnet No. 19   [Sonett Nr. 19]
BFA 14, 437; 1939; P1964; D.C.
Copyright © 1964 by Bertolt-Brecht-Erben / Suhrkamp Verlag

Then at the last, when death . . .   [Als es soweit war . . .]
BFA 15, 40; 1941; P1964; D.C.
Copyright © 1964 by Bertolt-Brecht-Erben / Suhrkamp Verlag

Wreckage   [Die Trümmer]
BFA 15, 42; 1941; P1964; D.C.
Copyright © 1964 by Bertolt-Brecht-Erben / Suhrkamp Verlag

Remembering my little teacher . . .   [Eingedenk meiner
           kleinen Lehrmeisterin . . .]
BFA 15, 43; 1941; P1964; D.C.
Copyright © 1964 by Bertolt-Brecht-Erben / Suhrkamp Verlag

In the ninth year   [Im neunten Jahre der
fleeing from Hitler . . .   Flucht vor Hitler . . .]
BFA 15, 44; 1941; P1964; D.C.
Copyright © 1964 by Bertolt-Brecht-Erben / Suhrkamp Verlag

My general has fallen . . .   [Mein General ist gefallen . . .]
BFA 15, 45; 1941; P1964; D.C.
Copyright © 1964 by Bertolt-Brecht-Erben / Suhrkamp Verlag

After the death of my   [Nach dem Tod meiner
collaborator M. S.   Mitarbeiterin M.S.]
BFA 15, 45; 1941; P1964; D.C.
Copyright © 1964 by Bertolt-Brecht-Erben / Suhrkamp Verlag

When I came back from   [Als ich ging nach
Saint-Nazaire . . .   Saint Nazaire . . .]
BFA 15, 74; 1942; P1956; D.C.
Originally written for the play *The Visions of Simone Machard.*
Copyright © 1956 by Bertolt-Brecht-Erben / Suhrkamp Verlag

Instruction in love   [Liebesunterricht]
BFA 15, 162; 1945; P1993; T.K.
Copyright © 1993 by Bertolt-Brecht-Erben / Suhrkamp Verlag

The song of fraternization   [Lied vom Fraternisieren]
BFA 15, 177; 1946; P1949; T.K.
This song is sung by the camp-following prostitute, Yvette, in later
versions of *Mother Courage and Her Children.*
Copyright © 1949 by Bertolt-Brecht-Erben / Suhrkamp Verlag

The plum song   [Das Pflaumenlied]
BFA 15, 192; 1948; P1950; T.K.
Written for the Zurich premiere of *Mr Puntila and his Man Matti.* Paul
Dessau set it to music on the basis of the tune of "When It's Springtime
in the Rockies."
Copyright © 1950 by Bertolt-Brecht-Erben / Suhrkamp Verlag

Sauna and sex   [Sauna und Beischlaf]
BFA 15, 193; 1948; P1982; T.K.
In his notebook Brecht signed this and another "pornographic" poem,
"Thomas Mann."
Copyright © 1982 by Bertolt-Brecht-Erben / Suhrkamp Verlag

Weaknesses [Schwächen]
BFA 15, 223; 1950; P1964; T.K.
Copyright © 1964 by Bertolt-Brecht-Erben / Suhrkamp Verlag

When I left you, afterwards . . . [Als ich nachher
von dir ging . . .]
BFA 15, 240; 1950; P1953; D.C.
Copyright © 1953 by Bertolt-Brecht-Erben / Suhrkamp Verlag

My love gave me a little branch . . . [Die Liebste
gab mir einen
Zweig . . .]
BFA 15, 240; 1950; P1953; D.C.
Copyright © 1953 by Bertolt-Brecht-Erben / Suhrkamp Verlag

Seven roses the rosebush has . . . [Sieben Rosen
hat der Strauch . . .]
BFA 15, 241; 1950; P1953; D.C.
Copyright © 1953 by Bertolt-Brecht-Erben / Suhrkamp Verlag

When it is fun with you . . . [Wenn du mich
lustig machst . . .]
BFA 15, 241; 1950; P1953; D.C.
Copyright © 1953 by Bertolt-Brecht-Erben / Suhrkamp Verlag

Smoke [Der Rauch]
BFA 12, 308; 1953; P1953; T.K.
The poem referred originally to the house that Brecht acquired for the
young actor Käthe Reichel, near his own house in Buckow.
Copyright © 1953 by Bertolt-Brecht-Erben / Suhrkamp Verlag

Love song from a bad time [Liebeslied
aus einer schlechten
Zeit]
BFA 15, 286; c.1954; P1993; T.K.
Copyright © 1993 by Bertolt-Brecht-Erben / Suhrkamp Verlag

Send me a leaf . . .   [Schicke mir ein
                                        Blatt . . .]

BFA 15, 293; 1955; P1964; D.C.
Copyright © 1964 by Bertolt-Brecht-Erben / Suhrkamp Verlag

When I have to leave you dear . . .   [Wenn ich von dir gehen
                                        werde . . .]

BFA 15, 288; 1955; P1959; T.K.
This was written for Brecht's adaptation of Farquhar's 1706 play *The Recruiting Officer* (*Trumpets and Drums*), where it is sung on the banks of the Severn, the first verse by a recruit, the second by his girl.
Copyright © 1959 by Bertolt-Brecht-Erben / Suhrkamp Verlag

ABOUT THE TRANSLATORS

DAVID CONSTANTINE is a freelance writer and translator. His most recent volume of poetry is *Elder* (2014); his fourth collection of short stories, *Tea at the Midland*, won the Frank O'Connor International Short Story Award in 2013. Among his translations are Goethe's *Faust*, *Selected Poems* of Friedrich Hölderlin, *Selected Writings* of Heinrich von Kleist, and poems and plays by Brecht.

TOM KUHN teaches at the University of Oxford where he is a Fellow of St Hugh's College. He works on twentieth-century drama and German exile literature and has been, since 1996, editor of the main English-language Brecht edition. In that role he has enjoyed a privileged overview of the translation and reception of Brecht's works. Major publications include *Brecht on Theatre* and *Brecht on Art and Politics*.

Together, David Constantine and Tom Kuhn are embarking on a major new edition of Brecht's poems.